Communication and Creativity in the Math Classroom

Previous Works by Nicholas J. Rinaldi
*The Math Teacher's Toolbox: How to
Teach Math to Teenagers and Survive* (2013)

Communication and Creativity in the Math Classroom

Non-Traditional Activities and Strategies That Stress Life Skills

Nicholas J. Rinaldi

ROWMAN & LITTLEFIELD EDUCATION
A DIVISION OF

ROWMAN & LITTLEFIELD
Lanham • Boulder • New York • Toronto • Plymouth, UK

Published by Rowman & Littlefield Education
A division of Rowman & Littlefield
4501 Forbes Boulevard, Suite 200, Lanham, Maryland 20706
www.rowman.com

10 Thornbury Road, Plymouth PL6 7PP, United Kingdom

Copyright © 2014 by Nicholas J. Rinaldi

All rights reserved. With the exception of activities, no part of this book may be reproduced in any form or by any electronic or mechanical means, including information storage and retrieval systems, without written permission from the publisher, except by a reviewer who may quote passages in a review.

British Library Cataloguing in Publication Information Available

Library of Congress Cataloging-in-Publication Data

Rinaldi, Nicholas J., 1945– author.
  Communication and creativity in the math classroom : non-traditional activities and strategies that stress life skills / Nicholas J. Rinaldi.
    pages cm
  Includes bibliographical references.
   ISBN 978-1-4758-0692-2 (pbk. : alk. paper)—ISBN 978-1-4758-0693-9 (electronic) 1. Mathematics—Study and teaching (Secondary)—Activity programs. 2. Creative teaching. 3. Communication in mathematics. I. Title.
  QA11.2.R558 2014
  510.71'2—dc23   2013033509

∞™ The paper used in this publication meets the minimum requirements of American National Standard for Information Sciences—Permanence of Paper for Printed Library Materials, ANSI/NISO Z39.48-1992.

Printed in the United States of America

Contents

Preface		vii
Introduction		xi
1	**Let's Begin at the Beginning**	1
	Opening-of-Class Activities	1
	Unusual Equations	2
	Three of a Kind	3
	Palindrome Puzzler	4
	Famous Structures	5
	How Observant Are You?	6
	Miscellaneous Brain Teasers	7
2	**Can We Talk?**	9
	You and Me	9
	Do I Have to Draw You a Picture?	10
	Joy Ride	12
	Oh, Say Can You See	14
	Lady Liberty and Me	18
	Talking Baseball	20
	To Serve a Serving	21
	Troublesome Technology	23
	Is Love Transitive?	25
	Student Presentations	25
	Do It Up Front	29
	Remember?	29
	Engaging Questions/Comments	30

3	Let's Create Creativity	31
	A Picture Is Worth a Thousand Points	31
	I Am a Geometric Figure	33
	I Am a Number	36
	Once Upon a Time	39
	Game Time	41
3.14	Happy Pi Day	43
	General Math, Prealgebra, and Algebra I Classes	44
	Geometry Classes	44
	Algebra II and More-Advanced Classes	45
	Name That Pi	48
4	In Search of . . .	51
	Geometry Scavenger Hunt	52
	Number Scavenger Hunt	53
	Transformation Treasure Trek	55
5	But Wait, There's Still More	57
	Linguini Lines	57
	W-o-r-d C-h-a-i-n-s	59
	Your Guess Is as Good as Mine	60
	Emergency Folder	61
	Random Students	62
	Take Me Out to the Ball Game	63
	Guess What's on My Mind	64
	The Equation of a Line	64
	It's a Sine of the Times	66
Conclusion		69
Appendix		71
Answers to Selected Exercises		75

Preface

As teachers we all have similar goals for our students. We want them to learn, not just the material in the standard curriculum, but also the skills they will need for the rest of their lives. Unfortunately, teaching math directly out of the book offers little opportunity for students to learn life skills, to learn with excitement, or to learn with a sense of adventure.

I have been teaching math for more than forty years. The overwhelming majority of the books I have used feature traditional, contrived, and somewhat boring problems and activities. They seldom engage students or allow the opportunity for teachers to introduce life skills into lessons. Consequently, over the years I created a multitude of my own problems and activities that emphasize life skills. I used them with my students, noted the results, received feedback, and made adjustments.

Communication and Creativity in the Math Classroom, a companion book to my first book, *The Math Teacher's Toolbox* (Rowman & Littlefield Education, 2013), provides the teacher with activities and ideas that are motivating, appealing, and engaging to students. The exercises emphasize communicating effectively, being creative, analyzing a variety of problems, following directions, and working cooperatively with others. These skills are very valuable yet are rarely covered in the traditional math curriculum. The varied problems, materials, and ideas in this book allow teachers to interject these skills into daily lessons while addressing a variety of mathematical topics.

Because you are reading this book, I assume you are a middle school or high school math teacher or someone who is enrolled in a teacher preparation program. Or perhaps, you read *The Math Teacher's Toolbox*, liked the strategies and materials, and are looking for more. Whether you are a new or an experienced teacher, *The Math Teacher's Toolbox* and this companion book, *Communication and Creativity in the Math Classroom*, provide guidance and serve as sources of topics, ideas, and activities. You will find, and more importantly your students will find, the activities and ideas to be appealing and engaging.

My previous book, *The Math Teacher's Toolbox*, has the main premise that a teacher has a greater chance of being successful if he or she has strong classroom management skills, including the teacher's ability to keep his or her students on task. One of the best ways to accomplish this is to present lessons and exercises that provide students with the opportunity to be actively involved in their learning. *Communication and Creativity in the Math Classroom* contains more ideas, problems, and activities to do just that.

My name is Nick Rinaldi, and for forty-one years I taught mathematics at Branford High School. Branford is a town on the southern Connecticut shoreline about ten miles east of New Haven. I am now retired from teaching in Branford and am currently an adjunct math professor at the University of New Haven (UNH). Also, for six years I taught an education course at UNH called Math Strategies in Secondary Education. This is a course for graduate students who are preparing to become math teachers. The course focuses on various teaching strategies and classroom management skills.

For the last twenty-eight of my forty-one years at Branford High School, I was the math department chairman. Part of my job was to observe teachers as they presented their lessons. Consequently, I worked closely with dozens of educators who displayed various levels of competency and classroom management skills. I saw a lot of good teaching along with a considerable amount of mediocre and sometimes even poor teaching. I noticed that as a result, too many students were turned off to math because of the way lessons were presented. A traditional approach, combined with conventional problems and activities, usually does not motivate students or enhance their learning, especially those students who don't like math.

During my teaching career, I attended numerous conferences, workshops, and conventions. From my experiences at these meetings, my personal work with teachers, reading many articles in various educational journals, and feedback from students, I came to the conclusion that ineffective classroom management is most likely the major reason teachers struggle or even fail.

This was my primary motivation to write *The Math Teacher's Toolbox*, the basic objective being to provide various tools to help improve classroom management skills and, as a result, raise the interest level of students and improve their learning. The ideas presented have been classroom tested and can be used in virtually any middle or high school classroom, although most of the activities and ideas included are geared to high school students.

As is the case with the materials in *Toolbox*, most of the activities and exercises presented in *Communication and Creativity in the Math Classroom* can be used in nearly every math course to supplement and enrich the mathematical themes being presented. Many of the activities can be used as assessments; therefore, suggested scoring rubrics as well as strategies and observations are included for your consideration. For your convenience, many of the materials are easily reproducible and ready to use.

These concepts and materials are presented to complement your teaching philosophy and style and to meet the needs of your students. It is up to you to decide how and when to use them effectively.

Introduction

Communication and Creativity in the Math Classroom provides a collection of ready-to-use, nontraditional activities and strategies that stress life skills.

Chapter 1 is analogous to the beginning of class. Here you will find opening-of-class activities that will mentally engage your students and put them into a thinking mode for the lesson that follows. Many problems require analysis. These are different from the opening-of-class activities presented in my previous book, *The Math Teacher's Toolbox*.

Chapter 2 addresses communication skills within the context of mathematical themes. Communication is one of the most important skills we can teach our students. In a math class, the opportunities to do this are limited. This chapter contains math-based activities that help students to improve their communication skills. For example, one of the exercises requires the students to use complete sentences and appropriate mathematical vocabulary to write a procedure to find the height of their school's flagpole. Also included are strategies and ideas to help you to promote better communication.

Chapter 3 provides activities that address creativity. One of the activities requires the students to choose a theme and then write a story using at least ten mathematical words or phrases. Their work must clearly demonstrate their understanding of the mathematical vocabulary used. Past practice indicates that students are very receptive to being creative, especially in a math class where the opportunity is rare or nonexistent.

The next chapter presents materials and activities to celebrate Pi Day, so the chapter is appropriately numbered 3.14. All of the exercises may be used on Pi Day, and some may be used at any time that you would like students to practice solving problems requiring the use of pi. The "Name That Pi" exercise can also be used as an opening-of-class activity.

Activities in Chapter 4 are scavenger and treasure hunts. These "hunts" require students to search magazines and other printed materials to find pictures or examples of math items on a list they are given and to discover the location of a "treasure" by carefully following directions and applying their knowledge of mathematical transformations.

Chapter 5 contains activities not previously mentioned in the book that have been successfully used in the classroom. Also included are strategies, techniques, and ideas to help increase your effectiveness as a teacher.

The appendix contains supplementary materials to some of the topics presented in an easily reproducible format.

Chapter 1

Let's Begin at the Beginning

OPENING-OF-CLASS ACTIVITIES

At the beginning of each class, you can stimulate the students mentally by giving them a problem that should engage their minds and help prepare them for the lesson. These problems also allow the weaker math students the opportunity to "compete" with the stronger students; the nonmathematical problems give *all* students a chance for success. Also, students enjoy doing them and usually have some fun.

Opening-of-class activities can take many forms, such as

1. Problems to introduce the next lesson
2. Problems to review previous lessons
3. "Real-world" math problems
4. Holiday problems
5. SAT prep questions
6. General "brain teasers"

All these categories are addressed in my previous book, *The Math Teacher's Toolbox*. Following are additional problems that may be generally classified as "brain teasers." (All answers are in the back of the book.) For problems with multiple parts, such as Unusual Equations or Three of a Kind, you can give the students several at one time, depending on your time constraints for that particular class. You can use these exercises on consecutive days until they run out or do them periodically over the school year. At your discretion, students can be rewarded with extra credit, pencils, candy, and so on for successfully completing the activity.

UNUSUAL EQUATIONS

Example: 2,000 = P in a T
2,000 = Pounds in a Ton

1. 26 = L of the A
2. 7 = W of the A W
3. 10 = C
4. 1,001 = A N
5. 12 = S of the Z
6. 54 = C in a D (with J)
7. 8 = P in the S S
8. 88 = P K
9. 32 = D F at which W F
10. 18 = H on a G C
11. 90 = D in a R A
12. 200 = D for P G in M
13. 8 = S on a S S
14. 3 = B M (S H T R)
15. 24 = H in a D
16. 1 = W on a U
17. 1,000 = W that a P is W
18. 29 = D in F in a L Y
19. 64 = S on a C B
20. 40 = D and N of the G F
21. 6 = W of H the E
22. 93,000,000 = M to the S
23. 9 = L a C has
24. 101 = D
25. 60 = S in a M
26. 7 = H of R
27. 5 = F on each H (or T on each F)
28. 40 = T with A B
29. 30 = D H S, A, J, and N
30. 1 = D at a T
31. 2 = T D (and a P in a P T)
32. 4 = H of the A

33. 13 = C in a S
34. 5 = S on a P
35. 20,000 = L U the S
36. 360 = D in a C
37. 60 = M in an H
38. 13 = B D
39. 3 = M
40. 2001 = a S O
41. 6 = F on a C
42. 32 = T including W T
43. 100 = L on a C
44. 3 = W M
45. 7 = D
46. 1,2 = B M S
47. 206 = B in the B
48. 6 = S on a H
49. 4 = S in a Y
50. 21 = G S

THREE OF A KIND

What do the trio in each set has in common?

1. trombone
   children's playground
   laboratory microscope
2. dentist
   dry run
   army camp
3. fish
   sheet music
   dieters
4. hunting dog
   compass
   scoreboard
5. dungeon

jewelry store
sequence
6. golf course
salad
environmentalists
7. car
stock market
computer
8. present
mouth
window
9. hair
atom
banana
10. baseball
horseshoe
salad
11. railroad
wild animals
music CD
12. beach
gun
turtles
13. open can of soda
pancake
bad singer
14. newspaper
tall building
book of fairy tales

PALINDROME PUZZLER

A *palindrome* is a word (or phrase or sentence) that reads the same from left to right as it does from right to left. For example, a palindrome that means "trick or joke" is gag.

For each of the following definitions/clues, suggest a palindrome.

1. Male parent
2. Eskimo canoe
3. Method of detection
4. Seen at the Indianapolis 500
5. To move up and down
6. To hit a baseball high in the air but not far
7. Small child
8. 12:00 P.M.
9. To direct to a source
10. Someone who can bring you back to life
11. Female parent
12. A firecracker that doesn't work
13. Something that turns or spins
14. Sound a small bird makes
15. Performances done by individuals
16. Numerical data (abbreviation)
17. An organ of vision
18. To sound a horn or whistle
19. A title of courtesy in addressing a woman
20. A job, especially a booking for musicians

FAMOUS STRUCTURES

1. This famous structure (no longer there) was located in New York City at the corner of River Avenue and 161st Street. Construction was completed in 1923, and since then it was visited by well over 200 million people. What is it?
2. This structure was built in the late 18th century on 18 acres of land. Very famous people have lived here. It has 132 rooms, a barber shop, clinic, indoor pool, theater, gym, and its own library. What is it?
3. It was designed by Frederic-Augusta Bartholdi and completed in1884. It stands 305 feet high and weighs 450,000 pounds. What is it?
4. It was built 221 to 204 B.C. It is 15 to 30 feet thick, about 25 feet high, and 1,500 miles long. What is it?

5. It has been estimated that the construction of this structure required more than 30 million hours of labor. It was built between 3100 and 1100 B.C. Today it is one of the most popular tourist attractions in Europe. What is it?
6. This structure was built between 72 and 80 A.D. It is about 144 feet high. It is basically in the shape of a huge ellipse, approximately 600 feet long and 500 feet wide. It had a capacity to hold about 50,000 people. It is one of the most popular tourist attractions in the world. What is it?
7. This structure opened on May 27, 1937, after four years of construction. It is painted orange and extends a total of 8,981 feet. What is it?

HOW OBSERVANT ARE YOU?

1. On a standard traffic light, is the green light on the top, bottom, or in the middle?
2. In which hand does the Statue of Liberty hold the torch? What does she have in her other hand?
3. What two numbers on a cell phone have no letters by them? Don't look!
4. How many matches are there in a standard pack?
5. On the U.S. flag, what color is the top stripe?
6. What is the lowest number on the FM radio dial?
7. North of the equator does water go down the drain clockwise, counter-clockwise, or straight?
8. Which way does a "No Smoking" sign slash run?
9. How many sides does a stop sign have?
10. Do books have even numbered pages on the right or left side? Don't look!
11. How many sides are there on a standard pencil?
12. How many hot dog buns are in a standard package?
13. On which playing card is the card maker's trademark?
14. How many curves are there on a standard paper clip?
15. Does a merry-go-round rotate clockwise or counter-clockwise?

MISCELLANEOUS BRAIN TEASERS

What Are They?

Two objects carry out the same function, yet one of them has thousands of moving parts and the other has none. What are the two objects?

You Don't Know Jack

In an ordinary deck of cards, there are four jacks. Two of the jacks have two eyes, and the other two have only one eye. How many total eyes are on the four jack cards?

You're on the Right Track

A nonstop train leaves Chicago heading for New York City traveling 70 mph. At the same time, another nonstop train leaves New York City and heads for Chicago traveling at 60 mph. When they pass each other, which train is closest to New York?

Sick Leave

Walter spent three days in the hospital. He was neither sick nor injured (nor dead), but when it came time to leave, he had to be carried out. Why?

Decisions, Decisions

From a single match, you must light a candle, an oil lamp, a wood-burning stove, and logs in a fireplace. Which would be the best to light first?

Chapter 2

Can We Talk?

Communication is one of the most important skills we can teach our students. In a math class, the opportunities to do this are limited. This chapter contains several math-based activities that will help students to improve their communication skills. Also included are strategies and ideas to help you to promote better communication.

Many of these problems can be used as assessments; consequently some suggested scoring rubrics are provided.

YOU AND ME

This is a good activity for the students to practice their communication skills while doing some drills on various topics. Let's say the topic is factoring trinomials of the form $ax^2 + bx + c$.

1. Begin by writing a trinomial on the board. Show the students how to factor it.
2. Now instruct the students to choose a partner, and let them decide which one will go first.
3. Write another problem on the board or choose one from the book or a worksheet. The student going first now factors the trinomial while explaining the procedure to his or her partner.
4. After a sufficient amount of time, display the solution for all to see. Students may ask any questions that they have.
5. Next, put another problem on the board, and the second person does the problem while explaining the solution to his or her partner.

This activity can be continued for a few rounds or for most of the class, depending on the type of problems you are using and how much practice you feel the students need. If desired, after a round or two, students can choose different partners.

DO I HAVE TO DRAW YOU A PICTURE?

This is an activity intended for use in geometry classes. However, by changing the drawing to, perhaps, graphs of various lines, this activity can be used in an algebra class.

Objectives

- To demonstrate the importance of using precise vocabulary when trying to communicate
- To show the value of listening carefully to what others have to say
- To practice using mathematical vocabulary
- To provide a change of pace from the traditional math lesson
- To have some fun

Directions

To begin, ask for two volunteers. One comes to the front of the room and stands behind the overhead projector or at the board, facing the class; call this student the *drawer*. The other comes forward and sits in one of the front-row seats; call this student the *speaker*. A diagram is displayed in a position where the drawer cannot see it but everyone else in the room can.

The speaker tries to get the drawer to draw the diagram exactly as it appears. The speaker may not use hand gestures or anything else except words. The drawer may not speak but must do exactly what the speaker tells him to do. The speaker may tell the drawer when he or she is doing something wrong and help to make corrections, again only by using words. Figure 2.1 is an example of a diagram that might be used for this activity.

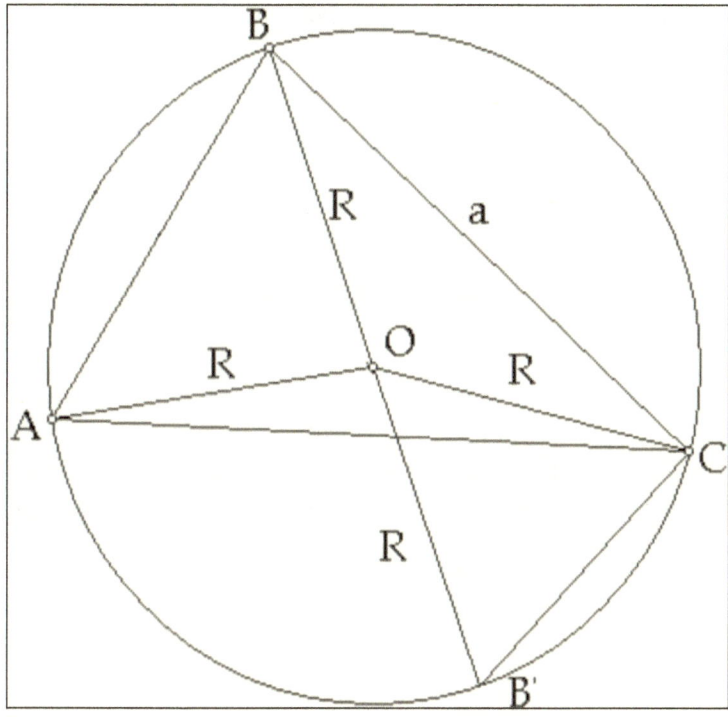

Figure 2.1.

JOY RIDE

Joy drives her car to work each day. The drive takes twelve minutes. Her speed at any time during one particular day is indicated on the graph in figure 2.2. On this day, several events occurred on her way to work. Your task is to write a paragraph explaining these events. Use the back of this paper for your story. Be certain that the rates of speed and elapsed times are addressed. Once you have completed your story, answer the following questions:

1. What was Joy's approximate average rate of speed from home to work? Clearly show how you arrived at your answer.
2. Based on your answer to question 1, what is the approximate distance from home to work? Show the math you used to support your answer.

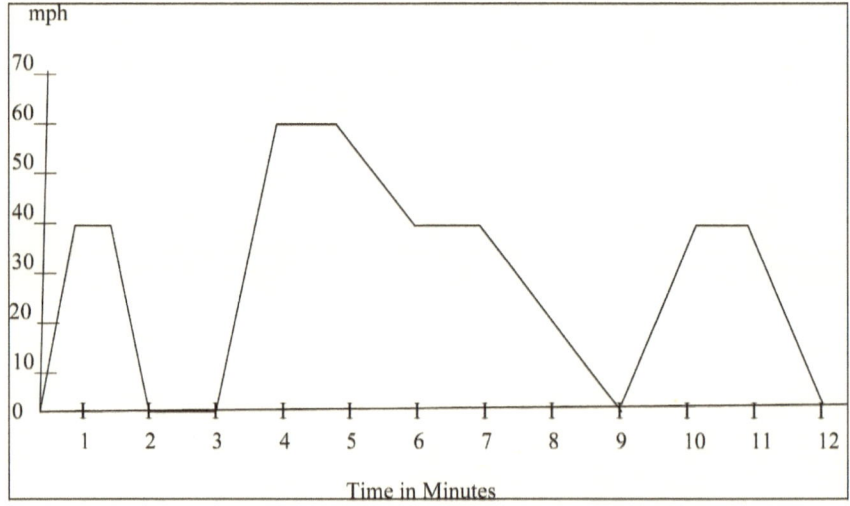

Figure 2.2.

JOY RIDE: SCORING RUBRIC

Name_____ Period_____ Date_____

	Possible pts.	Pts. earned
The entire story is consistent with the graph.	6	____
Response to question 1.	6	____
Response to question 2.	3	____
The story is well written (grammar, spelling, etc.).	4	____
The story is interesting/creative.	1	____
Total points earned		____

OH, SAY CAN YOU SEE

Here's an activity that is a change of pace from the everyday routine. It is intended for a trigonometry class or for a geometry class that has studied or is studying a unit on right-triangle trigonometry. Students may work in their regular groups (if you use them) or with a partner or partners chosen for this activity.

Objective

- Using a hypsometer and tape measure, the students will write a procedure that will enable them to calculate the height of the school's flagpole (or some other tall object).

Materials

- hypsometer
- tape measure (the longer the better)

Directions

To do this activity, you will take your class outside. Be sure to let a secretary or someone in the main office know the day and time you will be out of your classroom in case someone is trying to reach you or one of your students. It is also a good idea to put a sign on your classroom door explaining where you will be. The maintenance department can probably tell you the actual height of the flagpole. Before beginning the activity, plan on some class time for the students to construct hypsometers.

Constructing a Hypsometer

Materials

- a protractor
- a piece of cardboard
- a drinking straw
- tape

- some string
- a small object to provide some weight (metal washers work well)

On a piece of cardboard, trace a large protractor. Mark off the angle measurements at least every 5°. Using tape, attach a drinking straw to the straight part of the protractor. Punch a hole at point A and thread a string through it and tie a knot so it won't slip through. The string should be long enough to extend beyond the protractor. See figure 2.3.

The hypsometer measures the angle of elevation, which is indicated by where the string intersects the protractor. If you are looking straight ahead, the straw is parallel to the ground and the angle of elevation is 0°. If you are looking at something directly overhead, the straw is perpendicular to the ground and the angle of elevation is 90°. Use this hypsometer with the following activity.

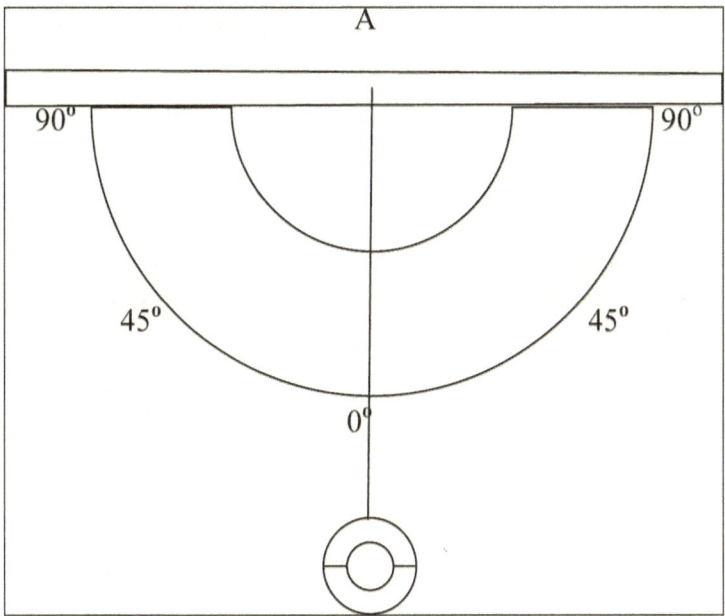

Figure 2.3.

OH, SAY CAN YOU SEE

Name _____ Class _____ Period _____

Objective

- To determine the height of the school's flagpole

Materials

- hypsometer
- tape measure

Directions

1. Please put your name, class, and period number on this activity sheet and the scoring rubric.
2. With your partner(s)/teammate(s), discuss the procedure you will use to solve this problem.
3. Then, *independent* of your partner(s)/teammate(s), in the space below, write out the procedure, using complete sentences and appropriate mathematical vocabulary.
4. Once outside, you may work with your partner(s) to take the necessary measurements.
5. Then, working by yourself, draw and carefully label a diagram based on the procedure you developed and the measurements you took. Write an appropriate equation based on the diagram, and solve it. Show work neatly. Use the back of this page if necessary.

OH, SAY CAN YOU SEE: SCORING RUBRIC

Name _____ Class _____ Period _____

Please attach this rubric to the sheet used to write the procedure and solve the problem.

	Possible Pts.	Pts. Earned
The procedure was clearly and accurately written.	10	_____
The diagram was correctly drawn and accurately labeled.	5	_____
The correct trig equation was given.	5	_____
The equation was correctly solved.	5	_____
The appropriate adjustment was made to reflect the height of the hypsometer above the ground.	2	_____
The work was neatly organized.	2	_____
The solution was reasonably accurate.	1	_____
Total points earned		_____

The following activity can be used when presenting a unit on ratio and proportion.

LADY LIBERTY AND ME

Name _____ Class _____ Period _____

The Statue of Liberty's nose, from the bridge to the tip, measures 4 feet, 6 inches long. How could you use a measuring tape and your own body to estimate how long her right arm is from shoulder to fingertip?

Directions

1. Use the back of this paper for writing your procedure and performing calculations.
2. With your partner/teammate(s), discuss this problem and the procedure you will use to solve it.
3. Then, *independently* write out the procedure, choosing your words *carefully*.
4. Next, do it; that is, follow your procedure to arrive at an estimate of the length of the Statue of Liberty's right arm. Partners/teammates may help each other with the measuring, but each individual is to use his/her own measurements to solve the problem.
5. Show all work/calculations clearly and neatly.
6. Express your final answer to the nearest inch (for example, 365 in., or 30 ft., 5 in.)

LADY LIBERTY AND ME: SCORING RUBRIC

	Possible pts.	Pts. earned
Directions were followed	8	_____
Clear explanation of procedure followed	6	_____
Calculations/work are neat and orderly	4	_____
Accuracy of solution	2	_____
Total points earned		_____

Notes to the Teacher

- The actual length of the Statue of Liberty's right arm is 42 feet, or 12.8 meters.
- With reference to accuracy of the solution:
  - Based on classroom performance by many students over several years, a percent of error of 10 percent or less is very good and should be granted the full two points for accuracy.
  - For a percent of error between 10 percent and 20 percent, one point should be deducted.
  - For a percent of error more than 20 percent, two points should be deducted.
- Carefully check the written procedures of those who worked together. Sometimes students will copy each other's procedure, although it clearly states in the directions that their writing should be done independently of their partner(s).

The following activity can be used in virtually any math class. It helps students to understand that everyday language is not always the language of mathematics.

Chapter 2

TALKING BASEBALL

The following is a comment made by a sportscaster about the famous centerfielder Buddy Baseball:

> Buddy Baseball is a 28-year-old centerfielder who gives *110 percent* every time he is on the diamond. His performance is *constant*. He is a great defensive player who *never* makes an error. With his *immeasurable* speed he can cover more ground than outfielders *half* his age. He also has *infinitely* more power than other sluggers; Buddy can hit the ball a *mile*. Last season he hit 50 homeruns while striking out only 75 times, giving him a homerun-to-strike-out *differential* of 2 to 3. After Buddy retires he is sure to receive *limitless* votes for the Hall of Fame.

With a classmate, discuss the difference between how the sportscaster uses the italicized words compared to how they are used in mathematics.

TO SERVE A SERVING

Name _____ Class _____ Period _____

According to nutritionists, to maintain optimum health, every day we all should eat at least two pieces of fruit and three servings of vegetables. Did you ever wonder exactly how big a serving is?

A serving can be defined as the volume of a tennis ball; in other words, if you stuffed food inside a tennis ball, that amount of food would be equivalent to a serving. But what is that in terms of cubic centimeters or cubic inches? Your task is to find out.

You will be given a tape measure and a tennis ball. In the space below, you are to write a step-by-step procedure that will explain how to calculate the volume of a tennis ball. State any formulas that you use, and be certain to use complete sentences and appropriate mathematical vocabulary. Once you have written the procedure, use it to calculate the volume of a tennis ball. Express your answer to the nearest tenth of a cubic centimeter or tenth of a cubic inch. Use the back of this page if necessary.

TO SERVE A SERVING: SCORING RUBRIC

Name _____ Class _____ Period _____

Please attach this sheet to the front of your project.

	Possible Pts.	Pts. Earned
A correct procedure was clearly explained.	10	___
Procedure was plainly written using appropriate vocabulary, proper grammar, etc.	5	___
Appropriate formulas were correctly stated and used.	3	___
The solution was reasonably accurate.	2	___
Total points earned		___

Can We Talk?

The following problem is intended for use in a geometry or trigonometry class. It can be used for classroom discussion, a team or individual assignment, or as an assessment to be graded.

TROUBLESOME TECHNOLOGY

Name _____ Class _____ Period _____

Objective

To help improve writing skills while using appropriate mathematical vocabulary.

You are in the computer lab working during your assigned time with the *Geometer's Sketchpad*, the interactive geometry software program. On the screen you have right triangle ABC, with C as the right angle (see figure 2.4). You are attempting to solve the triangle, that is, to find the lengths of the three sides and the measures of the two acute angles. Using the *Sketchpad* program, you are able to find the measure of angle A and the length of side BC. Suddenly the program freezes, and you realize that you must finish the problem in the next few minutes without the use of the computer.

In the space below, *clearly* explain how you would find the remaining three parts of the triangle. Use complete sentences and appropriate mathematical vocabulary. *Think before you write.* State appropriate postulates, theorems, and/or definitions to support your procedure. Use the back of this page if necessary.

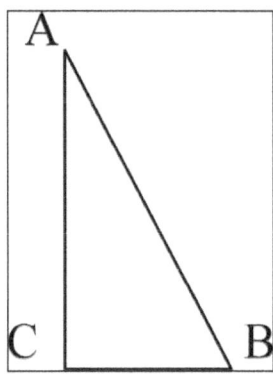

Figure 2.4.

TROUBLESOME TECHNOLOGY: SCORING RUBRIC

Name _____ Class _____ Period _____

Please attach this page to the front of your project.

	Possible Pts.	Pts. Earned
A correct procedure was explained to find $<$ B.	2	____
A correct procedure was explained to find AC.	2	____
A correct procedure was explained to find AB.	2	____
Procedures were clearly explained using appropriate vocabulary, proper grammar, etc.	2	____
Appropriate postulate, theorems, etc., were used to support the procedures.	2	____
Total points earned		____

IS LOVE TRANSITIVE?

In an attempt to stimulate communication among your students and to "humanize" algebra, ask this question to your class: "Is love transitive?" Pause a few seconds and then say, "If you think it is, put your thumb in the up position; if you think it isn't, put your thumb in the down position; if you don't understand the question, place your thumb in a position parallel to the floor"

Normally the overwhelming majority of the class doesn't understand the question. Explain the transitive property (if $a = b$, and $b = c$, then $a = c$), and then ask the students to work with a partner or in their regular groups (if you have them) to come up with an example to show whether love is transitive. Give them a few minutes and then call on the students for their answer and explanations. This activity often leads to an interesting discussion.

Follow up: "Which of the following comparisons are transitive?"

1. Is older than
2. Is taller than
3. Is victorious over (athletic competition)

STUDENT PRESENTATIONS

As a teacher you are continually communicating with students. Here is an activity that requires the students to communicate with you and their classmates by assuming the role of a teacher. Each student must write a lesson plan, present the lesson, and assign homework. This activity is probably more applicable to older students and/or a high-achieving class. The following materials were used with an advanced algebra class (juniors and seniors) but could be adopted to use with other classes.

(Note: In the appendix is a sample chart showing the assignment of dates when the students will make their presentations. It is probably a good idea to post this in the room or online.)

At your discretion the following materials can be presented to students in written form or simply announced to your class.

PRESENTATION EXPECTATIONS

You are required to make a classroom presentation on a topic from chapter(s) _____ in our textbook. Names of class members will be chosen at random. The first person chosen gets his/her choice of topics; the second person chosen then picks his/her topic, etc. So explore the topics and choose several in preferential order. Tomorrow I will pick names at random, and when your name comes up, be prepared to tell me which topic you will be presenting.

You will explore a specific section in the textbook and present the material to the class as though no one in the class has seen the material before. You may use outside sources (for example, other textbooks or the Internet). *Receiving help from another teacher is not permissible.* Your presentation will be graded by your classmates and the teacher. This activity will be scored with the same weight as a chapter test (100 points).

My expectations include:

- Handing in the *Presentation Form*, which basically describes what you will be doing the day of your presentation. This form is due the *day before* your presentation.
- Your presentation is to be at least 30 minutes long.
- You will assign homework to the class (at least three problems). You are also to complete and hand in to me the solution of each problem.
- You will present your lesson on the day that has been randomly assigned to you. If an emergency arises where you physically cannot give the presentation, the only options you have are to switch days with someone or to make the presentation to me (and any class member who wishes to attend) after school. If there is a need to switch days, please let me know as soon as possible.
- If classroom sets of materials are going to be used (for example, worksheets) in your presentation, I will need the originals *at least two days* in advance so that I will have time to make copies.
- If anything else is needed for your presentation (for example, scissors, colored markers, compasses, rulers, etc.), please let me know *at least two days before your presentation* so that I can arrange to have these items available.
- I am available to provide *minimal* help on the material you will be presenting. However, any *major* assistance you get from me for your presentation (like explaining major concepts) will cost you points.

PRESENTATION FORM

This form must be turned in the *day before* your presentation. Make a copy for your use.

Name _____ Date _____

Section Covered _____ Topic(s) Covered _____

1. What are the objectives of the lesson?
   _____
   _____
   _____

2. What teaching strategies/learning activities do you plan to use? (Suggestions: worksheet[s], group activity, game, calculator activity, etc.)
   _____
   _____
   _____

3. Attach an outline of your presentation. Include:

- Initiation—How will you begin/introduce the lesson?
- Lesson development—How will you sequence topics/problems/activities to meet the objective of the lesson?
- Closure—How will you end the lesson?

4. Attach a copy of the homework assignment with the solution key. All problems must be solved by you in advance. All work must be shown.

LESSON PRESENTATION: SCORING RUBRIC

Your Name _____ Date _____

Presenter's Name _____

Section Covered _____ Topic Covered _____

This form is to be turned in to me at the end of the class.
Circle your rating.

                                                                                       Poor   Excellent

1. The introduction to the lesson was "attention grabbing."   1 2 3 4 5
2. The topic was well organized and clearly presented.   1 2 3 4 5
3. Visual aids were effectively used to enhance the presentation.   1 2 3 4 5
4. The lesson was creative.   1 2 3 4 5
5. There was evidence of preparedness on the part of presenter.   1 2 3 4 5
6. The presenter used a clear voice and correct pronunciation.   1 2 3 4 5
7. The topic was explained using appropriate math jargon/vocabulary.   1 2 3 4 5
8. The assigned homework was appropriate for the lesson.   1 2 3 4 5
9. Questions from the class were answered with clear explanations.   1 2 3 4 5
10. The presenter's attitude was serious, confident, and enthusiastic.   1 2 3 4 5

Final Rating (add all the scores) _____

    The average rating by class members added to the teacher's rating will result in your final grade.

DO IT UP FRONT

Good communication usually begins with the teacher. The following is a procedure to help you to communicate with your students at the very beginning of class.

Before class begins, write on the board the objectives of the lesson or the topics to be covered in today's class. This puts each topic in perspective, serves as a guide to what the students will be doing, and helps them to follow along. For example:

Today's Lesson Objectives:

- To factor binomials
- To factor trinomials
- To factor special products
    o Difference of two squares
    o Sum and difference of two cubes

REMEMBER?

When beginning a unit of work, especially topics that you believe students may have already covered, you will find it is useful to know just how familiar the students are with the topic(s). You can save valuable time by addressing only those concepts that they really need to work on.

Let's suppose you are teaching an algebra II class and you are beginning a unit on solving quadratic equations. To know which topics you will need to spend time on, do the following:

List the topics you will be covering; for example,

- Solving quadratic equations by factoring
- Solving quadratic equations by completing the square
- Solving quadratic equations by using the quadratic formula

Ask your students to show you the appropriate number of fingers to indicate their familiarity with the topic. Tell them to hold the finger(s) close to their chests so that you are the only one who can see their response.

Say the following:

1. "If you are not at all familiar with the topic, hold up one finger." (preferably the index finger)
2. "If you are somewhat familiar with the topic but don't remember it very well, hold up two fingers."
3. "If you are very familiar with the topic and feel you don't need to work on it, hold up three fingers."

Now, by looking at the students' responses, you should have a better idea of which topics you need to spend some time on and which only need to be reviewed. If about half of the students are familiar with the topic, perhaps you can pair off the students and allow those familiar with the topic to teach those who are not.

ENGAGING QUESTIONS/COMMENTS

To engage students (or anyone else) in more meaningful and elaborate communication, you should try to avoid always asking questions that can be answered in one or two words. Try to include questions and comments that require the students to give a more complete response. Remarks such as the following ones should elicit more discussion and help improve communication.

- Can anyone offer a different point of view?
- What are some other examples?
- What are some of the reasons why . . . ?
- Explain what you mean by . . .
- Does anyone want to respond to that comment?
- Therefore, what conclusion can you draw from . . . ?
- What else?
- Tell me more about . . .
- Does anyone want to talk to _____ about . . . ?
- Can you expand on that?
- What do you suppose will happen if . . . ?
- What is most important about . . . ?
- What do we need to do next?
- Explain how you arrived at that conclusion.
- Can you think of another way we could do this?

Chapter 3

Let's Create Creativity

This chapter provides activities to help bring out the creativity in your students, a topic that is rarely addressed in the typical math curriculum. You may be surprised to see how imaginative some of your students can be when given the opportunity. Most enjoy these nontraditional activities, and several will probably tell you that they learned something about themselves by completing these exercises.

A PICTURE IS WORTH A THOUSAND POINTS

Correctly plotting points in a coordinate plane is a fundamental proficiency algebra students must master. Drill and practice with this skill is often tedious and not very enjoyable for the students. Following is an activity that is interesting to students and helps bring out some of their creative tendencies.

In this activity students are asked to plot a series of points (20 minimum) that, when plotted and joined together, form a picture. You can suggest that the students begin by choosing a theme consistent with one of their favorite hobbies or activities. Then they should draw the picture on a piece of graph paper. Next determine the coordinates of all the key points and list them.

This activity can be done as an extra-credit assignment, a graded project, or a classroom exercise. The activity is on the next page along with a suggested rubric.

A PICTURE IS WORTH A THOUSAND POINTS

Name _____ Period _____ Date _____

Objective

To list points that, when plotted on graph paper and connected, form a picture.

Directions

On a sheet of paper, page 1, you will have the following:

1. The title of the picture, which should suggest the theme. For example, you might entitle a picture of an airplane "Up, Up, and Away."
2. Directions to do the activity.
3. A listing of the ordered pairs (minimum of 20) using proper notation.

On a piece of graph paper, page 2, put the title of the picture and complete the activity; that is, draw the x and y axes, plot all the points, and connect them.
   Put your name on pages 1, 2, and this page, and hand in all three.

Scoring Rubric

	Pts. Possible	Self Rating	Pts. Earned
Title	1	_____	_____
Clearness of your directions (no. 2 above)	2	_____	_____
Organization and neatness	2	_____	_____
Accuracy	2	_____	_____
How well you followed the above directions	2	_____	_____
Originality	1	_____	_____
Total points earned			_____

I AM A GEOMETRIC FIGURE

Name_____ Period_____ Date_____

- If you were a plane geometric figure, what would you most likely be? A triangle? If so, would you be a particular type of triangle; for example, equilateral, isosceles, scalene, acute, etc.? Would you be a quadrilateral, such as a square, rhombus, trapezoid, etc.? Would you be a polygon of more than 4 sides? If so, which one? Or would you be a circle? Or something else?
- State the properties of the chosen figure in the space below (see figure 3.1), and explain why, based on these properties, this figure is like you.
- Now determine which of these figures is least like you. Again, explain why based on the properties of the figure you chose. Use the back of this page if necessary.

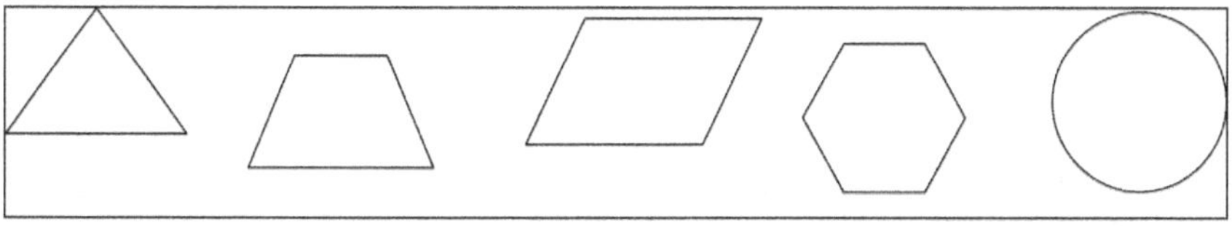

_____
_____
_____
_____
_____
_____
_____
_____
_____

Figure 3.1.

I AM A GEOMETRIC FIGURE: SCORING RUBRIC

A:

- The geometric figure most like the student is stated.
- The properties are clearly explained.
- Using the stated properties, the student presents a strong case as to why he/she is most like this figure.
- The geometric figure least like the student is stated.
- The properties are clearly explained.
- Using the stated properties, the student presents a strong case as to why he/she is least like this figure.
- Throughout the response, appropriate definitions, properties, vocabulary, and/or examples are used.
- The response is cohesive, well-organized, logical, and appropriate to the given task; response is free of digressions.

B: Criteria approach those of the A paper, but there are minor flaws in some areas.

C:

- The geometric figure most like the student is stated.
- The properties are explained but somewhat lacking in clarity; some properties may have been omitted.
- Using the stated properties, the student presents only an adequate case as to why he/she is most like this figure.
- The geometric figure least like the student is stated.
- The properties are explained but somewhat lacking in clarity; some properties may have been omitted.
- Using the stated properties, the student presents only an adequate case as to why he/she is least like this figure.
- In general, appropriate definitions, properties, vocabulary, and/or examples are used, but it is clear that a more thorough job could have been done.
- Generally, the response is organized and appropriate to the given task; response may contain some digressions.

D:

- In general the response lacks a clear or correct focus, or the focus is not maintained throughout the response.
- Overall, the response lacks adequate support with regards to appropriate definitions, properties, vocabulary, and/or examples; some of the properties or examples may be inaccurate or irrelevant.
- Response lacks organization or digressions significantly interfere with meaning.
- Ideas lack clarity and/or development; writing lacks fluency and/or transitions.
- Vocabulary, language, and mechanics are not appropriate for the purpose of the assignment.

F: Minimum or no effort is shown.

I AM A NUMBER

Name_____ Period_____ Date_____

There are several different types of numbers:

- Natural numbers
- Whole numbers
- Integers
- Rational Numbers
- Irrational Numbers
- Imaginary Numbers

If you were a number, what type would be most like you? What type of number is least like you? Write the definition of the types of numbers you chose. Then, using complete sentences and appropriate mathematical vocabulary, answer these questions and explain your answers. Use the back of this page if necessary.

_____
_____
_____
_____
_____
_____
_____
_____

I AM A NUMBER: SCORING RUBRIC

A:

- The number most like the student is stated.
- The definition is clearly explained.
- Using the stated definition, the student presents a strong case as to why he/she is most like this number.
- The number least like the student is stated.
- The definition is clearly explained.
- Using the stated definition, the student presents a strong case as to why he/she is least like this number.
- Throughout the response, the definition, appropriate vocabulary, and/or examples are effectively used.
- The response is cohesive, well organized, logical, and appropriate to the given task; response is free of digressions.

B: Criteria approach those of the A paper, but there are minor flaws in some areas.

C:

- The number most like the student is stated.
- The definition is explained but somewhat lacking in clarity.
- Using the stated definition, the student presents only an adequate case as to why he/she is most like this number.
- The number least like the student is stated.
- The definition is explained but somewhat lacking in clarity.
- Using the stated definition, the student presents only an adequate case as to why he/she is least like this number.
- In general, the appropriate definition, proper vocabulary, and/or examples are used, but it is clear that a more thorough job could have been done.
- Generally, the response is organized and appropriate to the given task; response may contain some digressions.

D:

- In general, the response lacks a clear or correct focus, or the focus is not maintained throughout the response.
- Overall the response lacks adequate support with regards to the appropriate definition; vocabulary and/or examples may be inaccurate or irrelevant.
- Response lacks organization, or digressions significantly interfere with meaning.
- Ideas lack clarity and/or development; writing lacks fluency and/or transitions.
- Vocabulary, language, and mechanics are not appropriate for the purpose of the assignment.

F: Minimum or no effort is shown.

ONCE UPON A TIME

Name_____ Period_____ Date_____

Your task is to write a story using at least ten mathematical words/phrases *correctly*. Pick the theme of your story from those listed below, or choose your own (please circle your choice). Your usage of each word/phrase should clearly demonstrate that you understand its meaning. Please underline or highlight the word/terms being used. Your story should be one or two pages long. You are to include some type of drawing, illustration, or diagram that addresses your story's theme. A scoring rubric is given below. Possible Themes:

- A favorite activity
- Your favorite holiday
- A memorable vacation
- Your favorite sport
- An interesting experience
- Other _____ (Fill in the theme of your story.)

The assignment is due on _____.

ONCE UPON A TIME: SCORING RUBRIC

Name _____ Period _____ Date _____

Please attach this page to the front of your story.

	Pts. Possible	Pts. Earned
Ten math words/phrases used correctly	10	_____
Neatness	2	_____
Directions followed	2	_____
Drawing/illustration	2	_____
Originality/creativity	2	_____
Story consistent with theme	2	_____
Total points earned		_____

Note: For each school day late, the project will be penalized 5 points.

GAME TIME

Most students enjoy playing games. In chapter 10 of my first book, *The Math Teacher's Toolbox*, several classroom-tested competitions and games are presented that enhance learning and provide the students (and teacher) with an occasion to have some fun. This activity gives the students the opportunity to create their own games. The objective is to create a game that can be used for learning, reviewing, or practicing skills in the classroom.

- Each student will work in a group of 3 to 4 students.
- Using classroom time, the students will meet to discuss the type of game they want to create: a game with a sports theme, a board game, a game that models a TV show, or anything else their imaginations can devise.
- Once the game is developed, students will write the procedures to be followed and rules to determine the winner.
- They are to advise you of any materials they need; for example, cardboard, dice, index cards, tape, etc. If the students are unable to supply these materials themselves, do the best you can in getting them.
- After the game rules and procedures have been developed, they are to be turned in to you.
- You then review their work and decide which game(s) are the most appropriate to be used in the classroom. Extra credit or some other reward could be given to the team(s) that created the best games.
- Then, periodically, the best game(s) can be played throughout the school year for learning concepts or for drill and practice.

Chapter 3.14

Happy Pi Day

Pi Day (March 14, or 3.14) is the only "holiday" that celebrates mathematics. If you wish to celebrate Pi Day with your students, you will find a complete agenda below. Please note that some of the materials can be used anytime during the year and don't have to be reserved for Pi Day.

To observe Pi Day, you can begin by making copies of the "Happy Pi Day" poster (see appendix) and displaying them throughout the building (cafeteria, library, hallways, classrooms, etc.).

- When your students enter the room on Pi Day, have the poster on the wall or display it on the overhead projector or from a computer.
- If you have a computer in the classroom, go to the website www.pi.ytmnd.com, where you will hear a voice singing the digits of pi.
- Next you can display the pi riddles and then the volume of a pizza problem on the overhead projector.
  - *Pi Riddles*
    - What do you call the ratio of an igloo's circumference to its diameter?

      Answer: Eskimo pi
    - What do you get if you divide the circumference of your pumpkin by its diameter?

      Answer: Pumpkin pi
  - Pizza Problem
    - What is the volume of a pizza with radius z and thickness a?

      Solution: Consider the pizza to be a cylinder. $v = pi\ r^2\ h$

      $\qquad\qquad\qquad\qquad\qquad = pi\ zz\ a$

Below are some Pi Day activities appropriate for various classes that can be done by students working in groups or individually. You can organize a competition out of some of these activities and reward the winner(s) with a small individual-size pie.

GENERAL MATH, PREALGEBRA, AND ALGEBRA I CLASSES

- Students will calculate an approximation of pi using a jar lid, a string, and a ruler. Have available several size jar lids; ask students to bring them in. The plastic types from a peanut butter jar, for example, work well. Have students use the string and ruler to measure the lid's circumference. Use the ruler to measure the lid's diameter. Use the formula $C = \pi d$ to calculate π.
- Bring into class various round items, such as dishes, pie plates, jar lids, pot covers, CDs, and so on. Ask the students to guess the area of each item. Then using the formula $A = \pi r^2$, have students calculate the areas to see whose guess came closest.
- Have students go online and find the first 100 digits of pi. Students will then determine the frequency of each digit and make a bar graph with that data.
- Have students list as many songs as they can think of that are associated with circles, rings, or anything round.
- Have students list as many things as they can that are circular (flat disk) in shape.

GEOMETRY CLASSES

- Explain to the students that they will be working in groups on Pi Day activities for the entire class. (If your students do not normally work in groups, they can be formed for this occasion.)
- Create as many work stations as there are groups. Position the stations in the room so that students can move in a predetermined order from station to station. At each station, written on a sheet of paper, is a problem that each group will have approximately five to seven minutes to solve. Each problem will require the use of pi in the solution. Choose appropriate problems from the textbook or other resources.

ALGEBRA II AND MORE-ADVANCED CLASSES

Again, these problems can be done on an individual basis or in groups. (Solutions are in the back of the book.)

1. What is the combined areas of two circles of radius 1 inch whose centers are 1 inch apart?
2. The diameter of a circular pie increases from 10 inches to 12 inches. What is the percent increase in the area?
3. As a sales promotion, the Sweet Delights Bakery Shop made a very large cookie, 24 inches in diameter and uniformly 2 inches thick. Three of the kids in the neighborhood began eating the cookie. If each has a stomach capacity of 252 cubic inches, will they be able to finish the cookie before they are full? Show work supporting your answer.

ANY CLASS

- Poster contest: Give the students a theme, such as circles in everyday life, and have them make a poster with that theme.
- Poetry contest: Give the students a theme, such as circles in everyday life, and have them write a poem with that theme.
- Prior to Pi Day, have your students go on the Internet to find facts about pi that are fun and/or interesting. Have the students write that information on a piece of construction paper or a large index card. Instruct them to decorate their card and bring it in to be put up on the room's bulletin board.

The following problems and activities are intended to be used with a geometry class. They can be used in an algebra II class or beyond as a review of geometry.

In this group competition, each group has to decide which members will work on which activities, which are: (1) calculating the answers to 4 problems that are posted on the walls of the room; (2) completing activities 5 and 6. (Note: At your discretion, these activities can be supplemented with or replaced by the "Name That Pi" activity.)

- At the end of the period, each team is to hand in the answer sheets (see appendix).
- The team that does the best earns a reward. (You can give each of the members of the winning team a small pie.)

These problems, or some similar to them, should be made poster size and taped to the walls in your classroom. (The answers to numbers 1–4 are in the back of the book.)

1. A circular in-ground swimming pool has a surface area of 452 square feet. For safety purposes, a circular fence is to be constructed around the pool at a constant distance of 6 feet from the edge of the pool. To the nearest foot, how many feet of fence are needed? Show all work neatly.
2. The circumference of a tree is 298 inches. To the nearest inch, what is the diameter of the tree? Show all work neatly.
3. A windshield wiper blade is 15 inches long. It cleans a sector-shaped area of a car windshield. The central angle of the sector is 85°. To the nearest inch, what is the area cleared by the wiper? Show all work neatly.
4. Assume the target in figure 3.14-1 has a bull's eye with a radius of 3 inches. The second circle has a radius of 7 inches, and the outer circle has a radius of 12 inches. Suppose darts were randomly thrown and hit the target 100 times. How many times would you expect the ring of the target marked B to be hit? Show all work neatly.

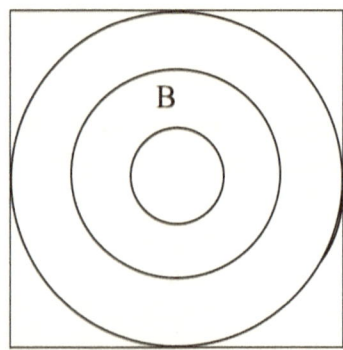

Figure 3.14-1.

Write each of the following statements at the top of an otherwise blank sheet of paper:

5. List as many foods as you can that are circular (flat disk) in shape.
6. List as many words (English) as you can that contain the letters *pi* consecutively and in that order. (Any misspelled words will not be counted.)

The "Name That Pi" activity should be reproduced, and one copy should be given to each team.

NAME THAT PI

Below are *clues* to words that begin with *pi*. The blanks represent the amount of letters in each answer.

1. 88 notes — _ _ _ _ _
2. pepperoni anyone? — _ _ _ _ _
3. a small flute — _ _ _ _ _ _ _
4. a miner might use this — _ _ _ _
5. a freshwater fish — _ _ _ _
6. don't fence me in — _ _ _ _ _ _
7. a former cucumber — _ _ _ _ _ _
8. let's eat outdoors — _ _ _ _ _ _
9. it's worth 1,000 words — _ _ _ _ _ _ _
10. to dawdle — _ _ _ _ _ _
11. 4 and 20 blackbirds — _ _ _
12. a part — _ _ _ _ _
13. a structure supporting the spans of a bridge — _ _ _ _
14. to pass into — _ _ _ _ _ _
15. beware of the big, bad wolf — _ _ _ _
16. park statues beware — _ _ _ _ _ _
17. coloring matter — _ _ _ _ _ _ _
18. touchdown! — _ _ _ _ _ _
19. found on the sides of the head — _ _ _ _ _ _ _ _
20. rice boiled in seasoned liquid — _ _ _ _ _
21. a heap — _ _ _ _
22. to steal — _ _ _ _ _ _
23. 1620 — _ _ _ _ _ _ _ _
24. small tablet — _ _ _ _
25. a qualified operator — _ _ _ _ _
26. I love green olives — _ _ _ _ _ _ _
27. teenagers hope this doesn't show up — _ _ _ _ _ _
28. this answer will bowl you over — _ _ _ _
29. fun at a party — _ _ _ _ _ _
30. a grasping claw — _ _ _ _ _ _
31. an amount grasped between the finger and thumb — _ _ _ _ _
32. to yearn — _ _ _ _

33. found in the tropics   _ _ _ _ _ _ _ _ _
34. pale red   _ _ _ _
35. the highest point   _ _ _ _ _ _ _
36. you're fired! (two words)   _ _ _ _ _ _ _ _
37. ½ quart   _ _ _ _
38. a spotted horse   _ _ _ _ _
39. Daniel Boone   _ _ _ _ _ _ _
40. having or showing religious devotion   _ _ _ _ _
41. a cylinder   _ _ _ _
42. Captain Hook   _ _ _ _ _ _
43. you're a nut   _ _ _ _ _ _ _ _ _
44. bang   _ _ _ _ _ _
45. an engine part   _ _ _ _ _ _
46. a round, flat bread   _ _ _ _
47. as black as   _ _ _ _ _
48. any small amount   _ _ _ _ _ _ _ _
49. home of Pirates and Steelers _ _ _ _ _ _ _ _ _ _
50. an unsuspected danger   _ _ _ _ _ _ _
51. growth hormone gland   _ _ _ _ _ _ _ _ _
52. to turn   _ _ _ _ _
53. dots on a video screen   _ _ _ _ _ _
54. sorrow for another's suffering   _ _ _ _
55. style or flair   _ _ _ _ _ _ _
56. New York Yankees   _ _ _ _ _ _ _ _ _

Chapter 4

In Search of . . .

Two of the three activities in this chapter are scavenger hunts. Students are required to search magazines and other printed materials to find pictures/examples of the math items on the list they are given. The third activity is another hands-on exercise. The task given to the students is to discover the location of a "treasure" by carefully following directions and applying their knowledge of mathematical transformations.

GEOMETRY SCAVENGER HUNT

Name_____Period_____Date_____

Directions

From newspapers, magazines, or original photographs, cut out a picture of a *real physical object* that represents *each* of the geometric figures listed below, *one photo/picture per object*. The object should be a representation of a *two-dimensional* figure, so it should be basically flat. For example, a coin is a good representation of a circle, but a basketball is not. Tape or glue the pictures on paper. Use as many sheets as necessary, and put as many pictures as possible on each sheet. *Arrange items in order* from 1 up; note where a term was skipped. Be sure to *clearly label* each picture with the number and the word or term you are identifying. *Clearly indicate the figure* by highlighting, tracing, etc. Also write a paragraph describing your opinion of this assignment and its value to you.

Scavenger Hunt Items

1. perpendicular lines
2. obtuse angle
3. acute angle
4. parallel lines
5. triangle
6. vertical angles
7. circle
8. trapezoid
9. kite
10. regular convex polygon (other than an equilateral triangle or a square)

Note: Items 1–5 and 7 are worth ½ point; 6 and 8–10 are worth 1 point.

GEOMETRY SCAVENGER HUNT: SCORING RUBRIC

	Pts. Possible	Pts. Earned
Listed point value for each item found and clearly identified.	7	_____
Directions were followed.	4	_____
The project was neat and organized.	2	_____
A paragraph was written.	1	_____
Total points		_____

This assignment is due on _____.

Please attach this sheet to your project.

NUMBER SCAVENGER HUNT

Name _____ Period _____ Date _____

Directions

From newspapers, magazines, or other printed resources, cut out a picture or advertisement that represents a real-world example of each of the types of numbers listed below. (*If you are not sure of the definition of an item, look it up.*) Examples might be pictures of road signs, house numbers, ads with prices of items being sold, nutrition facts from food items, etc. *Numbers from a book, like math problems or chapter or page numbers, are not acceptable. The number must be in content; that is the advertisement or real-world application must be included.* For example, just the fraction ½ by itself is unacceptable, but an advertisement saying "½ off sale" is acceptable. Also if you are trying to find the number 5 as a scavenger hunt item, submitting a two or more digit number that contains a 5 is *not* acceptable. *You are limited to one number per item.* For example, 7 could be used as a prime number *or* as a natural number but not both. Also, be sure the fraction you submit is actually a fraction. A store ad that says they are open 24/7 may look like a fraction, but it is not the indicated quotient of two quantities.

Tape or glue the pictures on paper. *Arrange items in order from 1 up to 10.* Use as many sheets as necessary and put as many pictures as possible on each sheet. Write "item was not found" next to any numbers where an example was not found. Be sure to *clearly label each picture* with the type of number you are identifying. Also write a paragraph describing your opinion of this assignment and its value to you.

Scavenger Hunt Items

1. decimal
2. proper fraction
3. percent
4. natural number
5. prime number
6. perfect square

7. perfect cube
8. improper fraction
9. perfect number
10. an integer that is neither positive nor negative

NUMBER SCAVENGER HUNT: SCORING RUBRIC

There are a total of 16 possible points. A point scale of how you will be graded is as follows:

	Pts. Possible	Pts. Earned
Each item correctly found and labeled is worth 1 point.	10	_____
Directions were followed.	2	_____
The project was neat and organized.	2	_____
A paragraph was written.	2	_____
Total points earned		_____

Please attach this sheet to your project.

In Search of . . .

TRANSFORMATION TREASURE TREK

Name _____ Period _____ Date _____

Objective

To use your knowledge of transformations and your ability to follow directions to find the location of a hidden "treasure."

A reminder: The translation <n, m> means the figure or point is to be moved n units to the right if n > 0 or | n | to the left if n < 0; this is to be followed by a vertical move of m units up if m > 0 or | m | down if m < 0.

1. Solve the following equations to find the coordinates of starting point A (x, y): $2x + 3 = 11$, $3y - 6 = 9$.
2. On a piece of graph paper, draw the x-axis and y-axis and plot point A.
3. Reflect this point over the y-axis; label the image B.
4. Find the image of B under the translation <-2,-1>; label this point C.
5. Find the image of C under the translation <2, -3>; label this point D.
6. Reflect this point over the line with equation x = 1; label this point E. (Incidentally, a translation followed by a reflection is called a *glide reflection*).
7. Rotate point E 270° counter-clockwise about the origin; label the image F.
8. Find the image under the glide reflection <3, 1> and y = -4; label this final point X.

If you have the correct coordinates of X, you have found the "treasure." Bring this paper and the coordinates of X and the completely labeled diagram to me.

Chapter 5

But Wait, There's Still More

This chapter contains activities, strategies, ideas, and techniques that have been successfully used in the classroom. Your students should find the exercises engaging, and you will find the ideas and strategies helpful in improving your effectiveness as a teacher.

LINGUINI LINES

Here is a hands-on activity that will give your students some practice with graphs of linear functions and the opportunity to discover properties of parallel and perpendicular lines:

1. Begin by giving each student a piece of graph paper. Instruct them to draw the coordinate axes in the center of the paper. If you have a transparency of a grid for the overhead projector, that would be helpful.
2. Give each student a piece of linguine (which is sturdier that regular spaghetti).
3. Tell your students that they will be given various properties of a line. They are to place the piece of linguine at the appropriate position on the grid to satisfy those properties.
4. After you have told them the properties, wait a few seconds and then place your piece of linguini on the grid transparency to indicate the correct placement.

Here are some suggested properties:

- A line with slope 3 and y-intercept -2
- A line with slope -2 and y-intercept 5
- A line with slope ⅔ and x-intercept 4
- A line with slope - ¾ that goes through the origin
- A line with a negative slope
- A line with a positive slope
- A line with a slope of 0
- A line with no slope
- A line with equation x = 4
- A line with equation y = -2

Now give each student a second piece of linguini and instruct them to do the following:

5. Place the two pieces of linguini on the grid so that they are parallel. Carefully determine the slope of each. What do you notice? Using appropriate mathematical vocabulary, write a sentence describing what you discovered.
6. Place the two pieces of linguini on the grid so that are perpendicular (form a right angle). Carefully determine the slope of each. What do you notice? Using appropriate mathematical vocabulary, write a sentence describing what you discovered.

The following are alternative approaches for numbers 5 and 6:

5a. Place one piece of linguini on the grid so that it has a slope of 3 and a y-intercept of 2. Place the second piece so that it has a slope of 3 and a y-intercept of -5. What appears to be true about the graphs? Using appropriate mathematical vocabulary, write a sentence describing what you discovered.

6a. Place one piece of linguini on the grid so that it has a slope of 2 and a y-intercept of -5. Place the second piece so that it has a slope of -½ and a y-intercept of 3. What appears to be true about the graphs? Using appropriate mathematical vocabulary, write a sentence describing what you discovered.

W-O-R-D C-H-A-I-N-S

Proofs in geometry and trigonometry identities are usually troublesome topics for students. Here is an activity that helps explain the linked nature of the steps in a proof or identity. Word chains should be initiated prior to a unit on proofs or identities and then can be used throughout the year as an opening-of-class activity or a classroom exercise. This is a good activity to include in an emergency folder. You might consider writing your own word chains or having the students write some.

Objective

- To transform one word into another by a chain of one-letter changes. (The best solution has the fewest words.)

Rules

1. Only one letter may be changed at a time.
2. Each change must result in an actual word.

Example: shame . . . scorn

shame
share
shore
score
scorn

Try these:

cat . . . dog
pig . . . sty
pier . . . dock
long . . . tall
heart . . . spade
ape . . . man
hurt . . . ouch
dusk . . . dawn

stone . . . blood
drive . . . shank

Possible solutions:

cat	pig	pier	long	heart	ape	hurt	dusk	stone	drive
cot	wig	peer	song	hears	apt	hunt	dunk	store	drove
dot	wag	peek	sang	sears	opt	hunk	dank	stare	grove
dog	way	peck	sank	spars	oat	husk	dark	state	grave
	say	deck	tank	spare	mat	musk	darn	slate	crave
	sty	dock	talk	*spade*	*man*	mush	*dawn*	plate	crane
			tall			much		plane	crank
						ouch		plank	crack
								blank	track
								bland	trick
								blond	thick
								blood	think
									thank
									shank

YOUR GUESS IS AS GOOD AS MINE

Here is an exercise that can be used as an opening-of-class activity to practice estimation skills or anytime you feel it is appropriate.

You will ask the students a question and request that they make their best guess at an answer; no calculators are allowed. Each student is to write his/her answer on a small piece of paper along with his/her name. After all have written their answers, collect the papers. The person who comes closest to the correct answer could receive a reward (extra credit, candy, a pencil, etc.).

Now you need to figure out the answer. Ask for suggestions as to how to proceed. Because the students have guessed the answer, most are eager to see how close they came and are more likely to suggest how to arrive at the solution.

Following are some possible questions:

1. How long would it take to count to 1 million at the rate of one number per second? (Answer: about 11.5 days)
2. How high is a pile of one million pennies stacked one on top of the other? (If 10 pennies are ⅝ inch tall, then the answer is 5,208 feet.)
3. If 1 million one-dollar bills were placed end to end, how far would they reach? (Answer: about 97 miles)
4. One million people are lined up with just an arm's length between each person. How far will this line reach? (Answer: about 530 miles)
5. About how many pennies would have to be piled one on top of another to reach from the floor to the ceiling in this classroom? (Answers will vary.)
6. How many pennies are there in one mile of pennies placed next to each other with their sides touching? (Answer: about 84,480)
7. How long would it take to spend $1 million at the rate of $100 every minute? (Answer: just under 7 days)
8. How many pieces of computer paper would it take to make a pile one foot high? [Answer: A ream (500 sheets) is 2 inches high, therefore the answer is 3,000 sheets.)

For some problems that can be answered quickly using just a tape measure, try the following: What is the width of this room? What is the length of this room? What is the height of this room? What is the distance from point A to point B? (Choose any two points A and B in the classroom.)

EMERGENCY FOLDER

As a teacher, you have probably had experiences with substitute teachers; sometimes they do an excellent job, while other times they can't seem to find the lesson plans you so diligently prepared. On other occasions you may have forgotten to leave the plans where they could be easily found, or perhaps they are not up to date, or possibly, due to an emergency, you are unable to get to your class and there are no lesson plans at all. In any case it is a good idea to have an emergency folder in your desk drawer that can be easily found by your substitute. A note attached to your schedule that is given to the sub by the front office is a good way to inform the sub of this folder.

Suggested materials include:

- Brain teasers (see opening-of-class activities). Because there is more time available for the students to work on these problems, they can be of a more sophisticated nature than the opening-of-class activities. Logic problems are a good choice to be included in this folder.
- Review problems for topics previously covered in the course.
- Problems/activities on fundamental topics in mathematics; for example, solving linear equations, graphing, factoring, working with exponents, etc.
- Extra credit assignments.
- Word chains.
- Materials from the Pizzazz series. Creative Publications produces a series of binders; as an example, one is called *Algebra with Pizzazz*, which contains exercise sets of problems compatible with concepts and skills found in traditional algebra books. Each page begins with a question/riddle that the student must answer by solving the problems. Each answer corresponds to a letter or words that lead to the answer to the question. For example, on the top of one page is the question, "What is a metaphor?" By getting the correct answers to all the problems, the student discovers that the answer is "To keep cows in." Yes, the answers are usually corny, but the students really seem to enjoy doing the exercises.

These Pizzazz booklets contain about 200 pages and cover a vast variety of topics that can supplement almost any algebra textbook. The booklets are expensive, so you may want to ask your department chair to buy one or two for the department and make them easily accessible to all department members. They can be used in virtually every math course for drill and practice or review. Go online and search for free worksheets and answers.

RANDOM STUDENTS

In some classes it is difficult to get students to respond to questions. Even when you call on them, some often say, "I don't know how to do that one" or something of a similar nature. Although it is controversial as to whether or not to reward students for answering questions, sometimes, with certain classes, it may be necessary.

Here's a procedure for your consideration. Tell the students ahead of time that you are going to randomly call on them. If a student gives a correct response, he/she will earn a point. At the end of class the student(s) with the most points will earn extra credit (or some other reward). To ensure all students have an equal chance of being called on, use the random number capability of the graphing calculator.

Assign to each student a number from 1 to how many students are in the class. If you use a grade book, use the number next to the student's name in the listing. On the graphing calculator (a TI-84 Plus in this case), select the MATH key, then PRB, then randInt(. Enter the number *1*, then a comma, followed by the number of students in the class, let's say 25. Hit *ENTER*, and a random number from 1 to 25 will appear.

Explain to the students that this is equivalent to putting the name of each student on a slip of paper and placing all the slips in a bag, shaking the bag, and drawing a name. By following this procedure you usually will not hear comments like "That's not fair, I never got called on." Names are chosen at random; consequently, each student has an equal chance of being selected.

TAKE ME OUT TO THE BALLGAME

A very important theorem in algebra is the zero product property, which states

If $a \times b = 0$ then $a = 0$ and/or $b = 0$.

Here are a couple of ways to improve your students' understanding of this theorem while having a little fun at the same time.

Say something like this:

> I am an avid Yankee fan. Any Red Sox fans in the room? I'd like to make a bet with you. If I win, you buy me an ice cream. If you win, I will buy ice cream for the entire class. Here's what we are betting on. The Yankees are so superior to the Red Sox that I bet that if we take all the runs the Yankees score this season and add them together, the total will be greater than all the runs the Red Sox score multiplied together. Of course we won't know who wins the bet until the end of the season, but who wants to bet?

Some students will be eager to take this bet, while others will see the reason that you are almost certain to win. Obviously, if the Red Sox are shut out, that is if they score zero runs in any game, then the product of all the runs they score throughout the season is zero. (Incidentally, baseball history tells us that it is almost a sure thing that in the course of a 162-game season, every team will be shut out at least once.)

This is a fun activity to use in April, when the baseball season begins. If the application of this theorem is not in your curriculum at this time of the year, you can use it as a review exercise; or you can wait to bring this up when you review for the final exam.

Here is an alternate approach to help students to understand the zero product property.

GUESS WHAT'S ON MY MIND?

Say something like this: "Let's see if you can read my mind. I am thinking of two numbers. When I multiply them together the product is 24. Can anyone tell me what one of the numbers is?" After some students give answers and a discussion ensues, most students will realize that they can't tell for sure what either number is; that idea is confirmed when you tell them the numbers you were thinking of were 72 and ⅓. Follow up the discussion with something like this: "OK, let's try it again. I am thinking of two more numbers. When I multiply them together the product is 0. Can anyone tell me for sure what one of the numbers is now?" At this point most students will say with certainty that one of the numbers must be 0. Either of these activities helps the students to understand the zero product property.

THE EQUATION OF A LINE

The equation of a line is usually a troublesome topic for students. The main problem is that they just don't understand what it means. Tell your students that the equation of a line gives the relationship between the variables. That is, the equation of a line tells how x and y (or whatever the variables are in the equation) are related. Using several examples typically helps the students to understand.

Crickets—Nature's Thermometers

By carefully counting the number of times a cricket chirps in 25 seconds, a formula (equation of a line) can be found relating the number of chirps, c, to the temperature in degrees Celsius, T, in the cricket's environment. That formula (equation of the line) is $T = \frac{1}{3}C + 4$. Because we have found the equation of the line, we now know the relationship between the number of times a cricket chirps in a 25-second period and the temperature in degrees Celsius in the cricket's environment. If we divide the number of chirps by 3 and then add 4, we have the temperature in degrees Celsius.

Exercise: Suppose a cricket chirps 63 times in a 25-second period. Based on the above formula, what is the current temperature? Answer: 25° C (or 77° F).

Fahrenheit to Celsius

Speaking of temperatures, there is a formula (equation of a line) that most students have probably used relating the temperature Celsius to the temperature Fahrenheit. That formula is

$$C = \frac{5}{9}(F - 32)$$

that is, this formula, or equation of a line, tells the relationship between the variables C and F.

Exercise: If the temperature is 68° F, what is the temperature on the Celsius scale? Answer: 20° C.

Bones, Bones, Bones

Forensic scientists tell us that there is a relationship between the length of a person's tibia bone (lower leg) and the person's height. The formula (equation of the line) is

$h = 2.738t + 67.868$,

where h is the person's height in centimeters and t is the length of the tibia bone in centimeters.

Exercise: You can have several students measure the length of their tibia bones and then plug that value into the formula (equation of the line) to see how accurately their heights are predicted.

CLASSROOM ACTIVITY

Working alone or with a partner, come up with situations for each of the following equations. Be certain to clearly define what x and y represent.

1. y = 0.25x + 14.75
2. y = 4x + 138
3. y = 75x + 32
4. y = -12x + 60

These examples and activities should help clarify what is meant by the equation of a line.

IT'S A SINE OF THE TIMES

When the concept of trigonometric functions is first presented to students, there is usually some perplexity on their part. For example, if they need to find the sin 30°, there is no problem punching the appropriate keys on a calculator and reading off the value of .5. However, most don't understand what the sin 30° really means and how the value of .5 is calculated. To help increase their understanding, you can begin by reviewing the concept of function. Draw a diagram on the board similar to the one in figure 5.1.

Explain that this is a function machine, and it will take the number inputted, perform the operations it is programmed to do, and then output the final value. In this example, when 5 is put into the machine, it is multiplied by 7, 3 is subtracted, and the final value of 32 is outputted.

Now, sine, cosine, tangent, cotangent, secant, and cosecant are also functions, but the operations performed by the machine are somewhat different. If the machine is programmed to take the sine of an angle, then think of it this way: once the sine button is pressed on the calculator, there is a program inside that constructs a right triangle with an

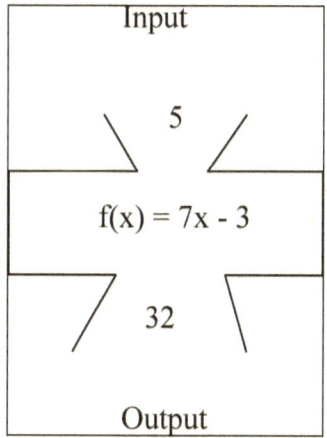

Figure 5.1.

acute angle whose value equals the angle inputted, let's say 30°. The calculator then uses the definition of sine and computes the ratio of the side opposite the 30° angle to the hypotenuse. Because a theorem from geometry tells us that all right triangles with a congruent acute angle are similar, the ratio is the same no matter the size of the triangle. Once given this explanation, students usually are able to make more sense of this initially confusing concept.

Conclusion

In this book you have been exposed to many activities, ideas, and strategies. Now it is time to try using some in your lessons. However, keep in mind that it is difficult to successfully incorporate many new activities or ideas over a short period of time. Remember, these materials were developed and implemented over many years.

It is suggested that you choose an idea or activity and try it with one class, preferably your best class. Tell them that you are going to try something new and that you would appreciate their input and honest constructive criticism. Then do it. You may find that implementing an activity or idea exactly the way it is presented in this book may not work for you. Consequently, you may want to make adjustments to fit your personality, teaching philosophy, and the needs of your students. Also, keep in mind that what works well in your period 2 class may not work well in your period 3 class. Successful teaching requires periodic analyzing and adjusting.

One of the great things about teaching is that if you try something and it doesn't go smoothly, you can analyze what happened, make the necessary adjustments, and try it again tomorrow, next week, next month, or next year. You really won't know which materials and strategies will work effectively for you until you try. If you slowly incorporate the ideas and activities in this book, you will not only be teaching mathematical concepts, but you will also be providing your students with engaging exercises that emphasize valuable life skills that are rarely addressed in a math class.

Appendix

This chart is part of the Student Presentations activity from chapter 2.

Table A.1. Sample Chart of Assignment Dates for Student Presentations in Chapter 2

Date	Section/Topic	Presenter
May 9	7-5 Solving equations containing exponents and radicals	
May 12	7-5 Solving exponential or logarithmic equations	
May 13	7-6 Natural logarithms	
May 14	Review/Quiz sections 7.5–7.6	
May 15	8-4 Simplifying rational expressions	
May 16	8-4 Multiplying and dividing rational expressions	
May 19	8-5 Adding and subtracting rational expressions	
May 20	8-6 Solving rational equations	
May 21	Review/Quiz sections 8.4–8.6	
May 22	Mimi-day Senior Exhibitions	
May 23	10-1 Graphing equations of conic sections	
May 27	10-1 Identifying conic sections	
May 28	10-2 Writing the equation of a parabola	
May 29	10-2 Graphing parabolas	
May 30	10-3 Writing equations of circles	
June 2	Senior class trip	
June 3	10-3 Using the center and radius to graph a circle	
June 4	10-4 Writing equations of an ellipse	
June 5	10-4 Finding the foci of an ellipse	
June 6	Review/Quiz sections 10.1–10.4	

Appendix

HAPPY

DAY

Appendix 73

PI DAY PROBLEM ANSWER SHEET

Team Name _____ Period ___ Date _____

For problems 1 to 4, show all work neatly below.

(1)   (2)

(3)   (4)

Answers to Selected Exercises

CHAPTER 1

Unusual Equations

1. Letters of the Alphabet
2. Wonders of the Ancient World
3. Commandments
4. Arabian Nights
5. Signs of the Zodiac
6. Cards in a Deck (with Jokers)
7. Planets in the Solar System
8. Piano Keys
9. Degrees Fahrenheit at which Water Freezes
10. Holes on a Golf Course
11. Degrees in a Right Angle
12. Dollars for Passing Go in Monopoly
13. Sides on a Stop Sign
14. Blind Mice (See How They Run)
15. Hours in a Day
16. Wheel on a Unicycle
17. Words that a Picture is Worth
18. Days in February in a Leap Year
19. Squares on a Checkerboard (or Chessboard)
20. Days and Nights of the Great Flood
21. Wives of Henry the Eight
22. Miles to the Sun

23. Lives a Cat has
24. Dalmatians
25. Seconds in a Minute
26. Hills of Rome
27. Fingers on each Hand (or Toes on each Foot)
28. Thieves with Ali Baba
29. Days Has September, April, June, and November
30. Day at a Time
31. Turtle Doves (and a Partridge in a Pear Tree)
32. Horsemen of the Apocalypse
33. Cards in a Suit
34. Sides on a Pentagon
35. Leagues Under the Sea
36. Degrees in a Circle
37. Minutes in an Hour
38. Baker's Dozen
39. Musketeers
40. A Space Odyssey
41. Faces on a Cube
42. Teeth including Wisdom Teeth
43. Legs on a Centipede
44. Wise Men
45. Dwarfs
46. Buckle My Shoe
47. Bones in the Body
48. Sides on a Hexagon
49. Seasons in a Year
50. Gun Salute

Three of a Kind

1. Slide
2. Drill
3. Scales
4. Points
5. Chains
6. Greens

Answers to Selected Exercises

7. They all crash
8. You open them
9. They are all associated with the word *split*
10. They are all tossed
11. They all have or leave tracks
12. Shells
13. They are all flat
14. They all have stories

Palindrome Puzzler

1. dad
2. kayak
3. radar
4. racecar
5. bob
6. pop
7. tot
8. noon
9. refer
10. reviver
11. mom
12. dud
13. rotator
14. peep
15. solos
16. stats
17. eye
18. toot
19. madam
20. gig

Famous Structures

1. The Old Yankee Stadium
2. The White House
3. Statue of Liberty

4. Great Wall Of China
5. Stonehenge
6. The Roman Coliseum
7. The Golden Gate Bridge

How Observant Are You?

1. bottom
2. right; book
3. 1, 0
4. 20
5. red
6. 88
7. clockwise
8. toward bottom right
9. 8
10. left
11. 6
12. 8
13. ace of spades
14. 3
15. counter-clockwise

Miscellaneous Brain Teasers

What Are They?

An hourglass and a sun dial

You Don't Know Jack

Because each jack has two faces, the total number of eyes is 12.

You're on the Right Track

When they meet, they will be in the same spot, so they will be the same distance from New York.

Sick Leave

Walter is a newborn baby.

Decisions, Decisions

The match

CHAPTER 2

Joy Ride

1. Joy's rate of speed from home to work can be estimated by averaging her speed over one-minute intervals.
From 0 to 1 minute: 20 mph
From 1 to 2 minutes: 30 mph
From 2 to 3 minutes: 0 mph
From 3 to 4 minutes: 30 mph
From 4 to 5 minutes: 60 mph
From 5 to 6 minutes: 50 mph
From 6 to 7 minutes: 40 mph
From 7 to 8 minutes: 30 mph
From 8 to 9 minutes: 10 mph
From 9 to 10 minutes: 20 mph
From 10 to 11 minutes: 40 mph
From 11 to 12 minutes: 20 mph
The average of these averages is about 29 mph.

2. Because $r \times t = d$

    $29 \times (\frac{12}{60}) = d$
    The distance from home to work is about 5.8 miles.

To Serve a Serving

Using the tape measure, the circumference of the tennis ball is easily found. Using the formula $C = 2\pi r$, the radius can be calculated. The volume can then be determined by using the formula $V = \frac{4}{3}\pi r^3$.

According to information obtained on the Internet, a tennis ball must be between 6.25 and 6.57 centimeters in diameter, that is, 3.125 and 3.285 centimeters radius. Using 3.2 as the average and the formula for the volume of a sphere, the solution looks like this:

$V = (\frac{4}{3})\pi r^3$
$V = (\frac{4}{3})\pi(3.2)^3$ using the π key on the calculator
$V =$ about 137.3 Note: If 3.14 is used for π, $V =$ about 137.2

Therefore a serving of vegetables is about 137.3 cubic centimeters (or about 9.2 cubic inches).

CHAPTER 3.14

For Algebra II and More Advanced Classes

1. Combined area = area of two circles – area of two triangles – area four segments.

   2π $\quad - \quad$ $\dfrac{2\sqrt{3}}{4}$ $\quad - \quad$ $4(\dfrac{\pi}{6} - \dfrac{\sqrt{3}}{4})$

   $2(3.14)$ $\quad - \quad$ $.866$ $\quad - \quad$ $.361$ $\qquad = 5.053$ in^2

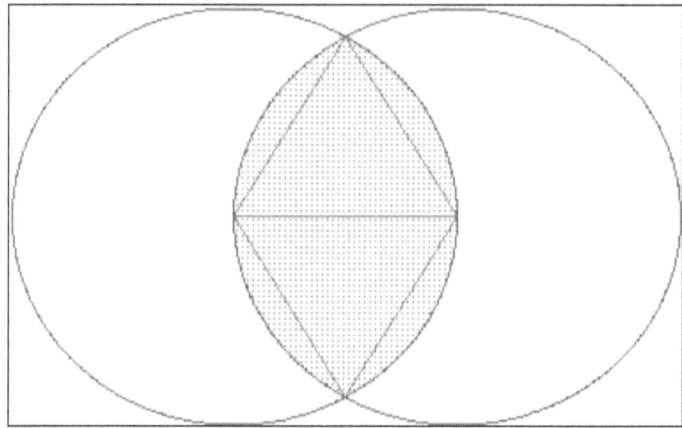

Figure 3.14-2.

2. Original area $= \pi r^2 = \pi \times 5^2 = 25\pi$

   New area $= \pi r^2 = \pi \times 6^2 = 36\pi$

   Percent of increase $= \dfrac{|\text{new}-\text{old}|}{\text{old}}$

   $= \dfrac{|36\pi - 25\pi|}{25\pi}$

   $= \dfrac{11\pi}{25\pi}$

   $= 44\%$

3. Consider the cookie to be a cylinder.
   $V = \pi r^2 h$
   $= \pi \times 12^2 \times 2$ using the π key on the calculator
   $= 905$ in³ Note: if 3.14 is used for π, V = 904
   Because the combined stomach capacity is $3 \times 252 = 756$, the answer is no.

Problem Sheet for Geometry Classes

1. About 113 feet
2. About 95 inches
3. About 167 square inches
4. About 28 times

Name That Pi

1. piano
2. pizza
3. piccolo
4. pick
5. pike
6. picket
7. pickle
8. picnic
9. picture

10. piddle
11. pie
12. piece
13. pier
14. pierce
15. pigs
16. pigeon
17. pigment
18. pigskin
19. pigtails
20. pilaf
21. pile
22. pilfer
23. pilgrims
24. pill
25. pilot
26. pimento
27. pimple
28. pins
29. piñata
30. pincer
31. pinch
32. pine
33. pineapple
34. pink
35. pinnacle
36. pink slip
37. pint
38. pinto
39. pioneer
40. pious
41. pipe
42. pirate
43. pistachio
44. pistol
45. piston
46. pita

47. pitch
48. pittance
49. Pittsburgh
50. pitfall
51. pituitary
52. pivot
53. pixels
54. pity
55. pizzazz
56. pinstripes

CHAPTER 4

Transformation Treasure Trek

These are the coordinates of each of the points in the activity:

A: (4, 5)
B: (-4, 5)
C: (-6, 4)
D: (-4, 1)
E: (6, 1)
F: (1, -6)
X: (4, -3)

www.ingramcontent.com/pod-product-compliance
Lightning Source LLC
Chambersburg PA
CBHW021215240426
43672CB00026B/322